WORKBOOK

Photography ~ Spring 2012

Publisher/Owner ~	**BILL DANIELS**
Advertising Sales Director ~	**SUZANNE SEMNACHER**
Advertising Sales ~	**LINDA LEVY**
	MARY PREUSSEL
	LORI WATSON
Design Director ~	**ANITA ATENCIO**
Director of Production ~	**PAUL SEMNACHER**
Online Portfolio Manager ~	**KIRSTEN LARSON**
Social Media Manager ~	**WILL DANIELS**
Directory Manager ~	**ANGELICA VINTHER**
Directory Marketing Manager ~	**JOHN NIXON**
Directory Verifiers ~	**AURELIO FARRELL II**
	JORDAN LACEY
	DAVID PAVAO
	ANGELA PERKINS
Technology ~	**JIM HUDAK**
	STEPHEN CHIANG
	RYAN ADLAF
Finance ~	**ALLAN GALLANT**
	EDUARDO CHEVEZ
Security ~	**MR. "T"**

WORKBOOK

in print. online. workbook works.

Production Specialist Portfolios

PORTFOLIO
Kim Healy Pretti
Prop Stylist

Production Specialists: Prop Stylists • Set Designers • Studio & Stage Rentals • Wardrobe Stylists • Location Finders
CGI Services & Retouchers • Production Services • Food Stylists & Home Economists • Hair & Make-up Artists

workbook.com/production

34

~ Contents

see the workbook on the go
MOBILE.WORKBOOK.COM

download the iPhone app at
WORKBOOK.COM/IPHONE

participate in our
BLOG

follow us on
TWITTER

like us on
FACEBOOK

connect with us on
LINKEDIN

workbook.com/social
in print. online. workbook works.

~ **Index**

*Artist's Representative

~ Index

*Artist's Representative

*Artist's Representative

*Artist's Representative

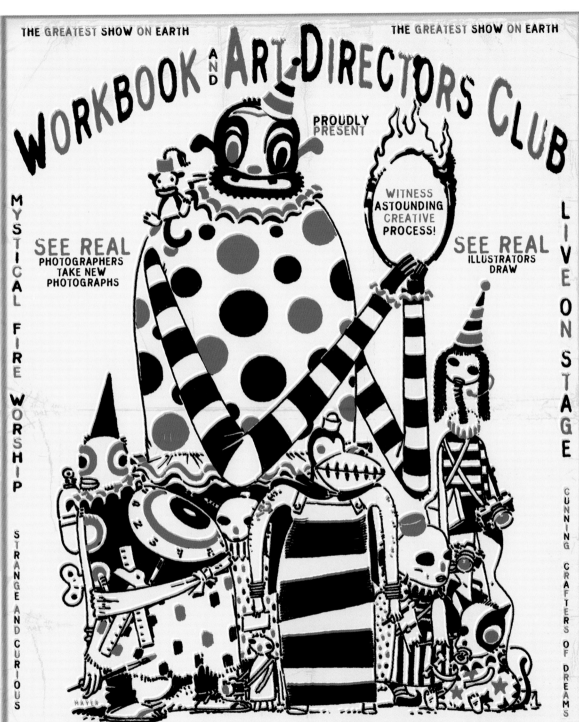

THE GREATEST SHOW ON EARTH

THE GREATEST SHOW ON EARTH

WORKBOOK AND ART DIRECTORS CLUB

PROUDLY PRESENT

WITNESS ASTOUNDING CREATIVE PROCESS!

SEE REAL PHOTOGRAPHERS TAKE NEW PHOTOGRAPHS

SEE REAL ILLUSTRATORS DRAW

MYSTICAL FIRE WORSHIP

STRANGE AND CURIOUS

LIVE ON STAGE

CUNNING CRAFTERS OF DREAMS

MAYER

CREATIVE CARNIVAL

WITNESS LIVE ARTISTS AND PURCHASE THE WORK RIGHT OFF THE WALLS

check your inbox or workbook.com/blog for the next big show near you

~ Photography

doss

LAURA DOSS PHOTOGRAPHY

schafrick

U.S.A	CANADA	EUROPE
ray brown \| REP	arlene evidente \| REP	bogna brock \| REP
+1 212 243 5057	+1 416 823 1713	+49 (0) 211 325 175

214.718.7745

terri glanger

LisaAdamsPhotography.com

also see directors section on website ▶

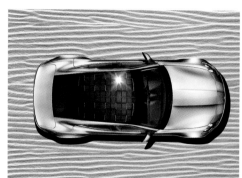

AH 212.431.5117 **www.andersonhopkins.com** blog.andersonhopkins.com

artists represented by **ANDERSON HOPKINS**

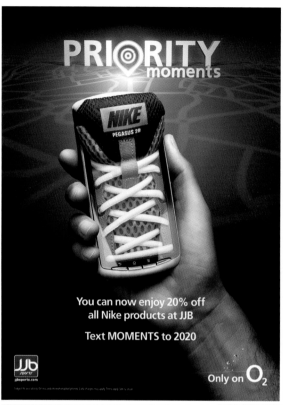

AH 212.431.5117 www.andersonhopkins.com blog.andersonhopkins.com

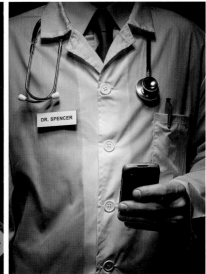

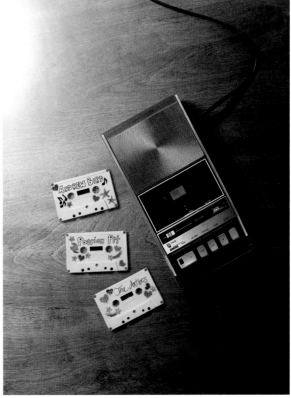

also see directors section on website ▶

also see directors section on website ▶

AH 212.431.5117 **www.andersonhopkins.com** blog.andersonhopkins.com

e-resources 4
e-search 3
e-clients 2
e-accounts 1
 0

artists represented by **ANDERSON HOPKINS**

Form AND *Function* MEET.
AND BEGIN A TORRID AFFAIR.

Simply More.

CIVIC Si

civic.honda.com

» THE LEGEND IS BACK.

MINI MAKES A RETURN TO RALLYING.

Following its legendary success in the 60s MINI is regaining its position in motor racing's premier competition. Ever since May, the MINI John Cooper Works WRC has been causing quite a stir in the World Rally Championship. We look forward to seeing all our fans once again. **www.MINImotorsport.com**

THE LIVING MOTORSPORT LEGEND.

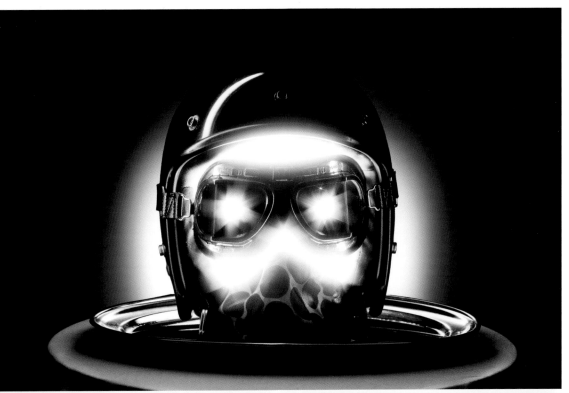

BRETT NADAL
—

via jim hanson artist agent ltd.
jimhanson.com

NOZICKA

STEVE NOZICKA PHOTOGRAPHY 314 WEST INSTITUTE PLACE CHICAGO, IL 60610

P)312-787-8925 nozicka.com nozickas@aol.com

JILL BROUSSARD
PHOTOGRAPHY

The Photo Division 214.763.5887 m@thephotodivision.com

Noel
Barnhurst
PHOTOGRAPHER

Noel **Barnhurst**
PHOTOGRAPHER

CANDACE GELMAN
& ASSOCIATES

SF 415-897-0808 **CANDACEGELMAN.COM**
CH 312-266-0808
NY 212-666-0808

RENDERUNIT
RENDERUNIT.COM
805-658-2224

CANDACEGELMAN.COM
415-897-0808

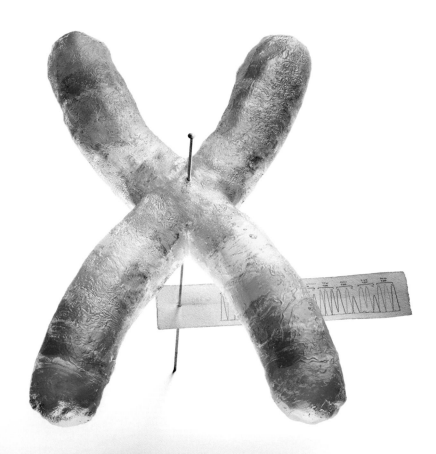

CANDACEGELMAN.COM

ellie
kingsbury
612.865.7063
kingsburypictures.com

JAY SCOTT BAKER

represented by

FosterReps.com
314.909.7377

WILD
TURKEY
AMERICAN
HONEY

EXCEPTI

ScottFerguson

ScottFerguson

MATT
HAWTHORNE
PHOTOGRAPHY

JEN BUTTERS
AGENCY
972.385.0078 DALLAS
323.308.9223 LOS ANGELES
MATTHAWTHORNE.COM

TALLGRASSPICTURES
PRINT // BROADCAST // MOBILE

JEFFREYLAMONT**BROWN**
photographer // director

619.227.2701 | jb@jeffreybrown.com | tallgrasspictures.com
PAULA GREN REPS 415.550.2441

GREG**W**HITAKER

represented by Holly Hahn 312 371 0500 gregwhitaker.com

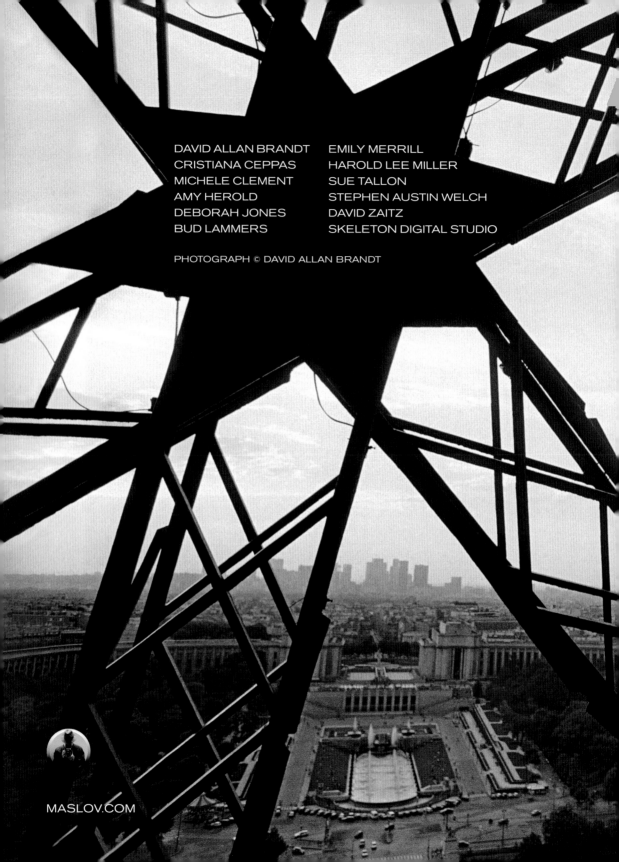

DAVID ALLAN BRANDT
CRISTIANA CEPPAS
MICHELE CLEMENT
AMY HEROLD
DEBORAH JONES
BUD LAMMERS

EMILY MERRILL
HAROLD LEE MILLER
SUE TALLON
STEPHEN AUSTIN WELCH
DAVID ZAITZ
SKELETON DIGITAL STUDIO

PHOTOGRAPH © DAVID ALLAN BRANDT

NORMAN MASLOV
AGENT INTERNATIONALE

Lisa Button 312 399-2522 Mid & Southwest buttonrepresents.com

Norman Maslov Agent Internationale 415 641-4376 maslov.com haroldleemiller.com

Lisa Button 312 399-2522 Mid & Southwest buttonrepresents.com

haroldleemiller.com Norman Maslov Agent Internationale 415 641-4376 maslov.com

CRISTIANA CEPPAS

 Norman Maslov Agent Internationale 415 641-4376 maslov.com cristianaceppas.com

emilymerrill.com Norman Maslov Agent Internationale 415 641-4376 maslov.com

DAVID ZAITZ

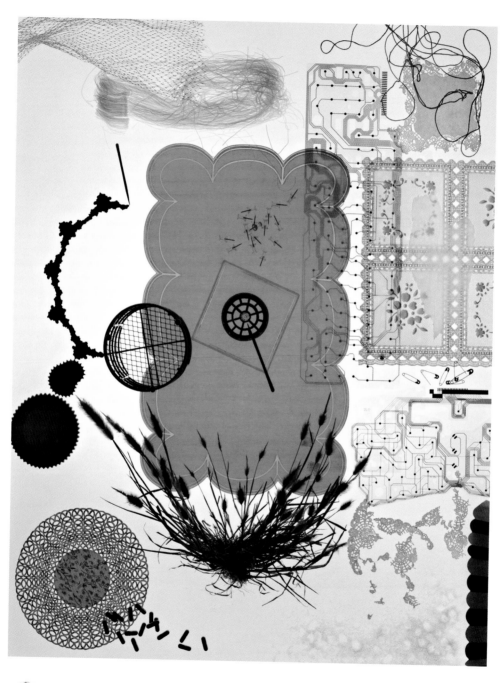

Norman Maslov Agent Internationale 415 641-4376 maslov.com suetallon.com

 Norman Maslov Agent Internationale 415 641-4376 maslov.com micheleclement.com

micheleclement.com Norman Maslov Agent Internationale 415 641-4376 maslov.com

Norman Maslov Agent Internationale 415 641-4376 maslov.com davidallanbrandt.com

davidallanbrandt.com Norman Maslov Agent Internationale 415 641-4376 maslov.com

SCIORTINO

Jeff Sciortino Photography
764 N. Milwaukee
Chicago, IL 60622
312.829.6112
www.jeffsciortino.com

Represented by: Jodie Zeitler
312.467.9220
www.jodiezeitler.com

SCIORTINO

Jeff Sciortino Photography
764 N. Milwaukee Ave.
Chicago, IL 60622
312.829.6112
www.jeffsciortino.com

Represented by: Jodie Zeitler
312.467.9220
www.jodiezeitler.com

312.751.9630
www.scottpayne.com

www.colinmcguire.com

colin mcguire photographs

t 614.975.0025

e info@colinmcguire.com

Represented by Jodie Zeitler
312.467.9220
jodie@jodiezeitler.com

145

MICHAEL**MAES**

SARAH DERER | EXECUTIVE PRODUCER | T 312 997 2775 | C 312 952 2770
MAESSTUDIO.COM

www.andreamandel.com

andrea mandel

grubman.

Steve Grubman Photography, Inc.
312 226-2272
www.grubman.com
Represented by
Carolyn Somlo Talent 312 209-8042
Stock available

N 50° 45.646' W 111° 30.084'

MICHAEL BOONE

PHOTOGRAPHY

312-890-3171

LARRY BARTHOLOMEW

COOLIFE

COLETTE DE BARROS

SHANNON GREER

PHILIP HARVEY

CHRIS KILKUS

Alyssa Pizer
MANAGEMENT

ALYSSAPIZER.COM • ALYSSA@ALYSSAPIZER.COM • 310.440.3930

ON DIAZ

CHEYENNE ELLIS

WILLIAM GARRETT

OSEPH MONTEZINOS

BETH STUDENBERG

Alyssa Pizer
MANAGEMENT

Follow us on:

facebook.com/alyssapizermanagement
twitter.com/alyssapizer
alyssapizer.com/blog/

LARRY
BARTHOLOMEW
PHOTOGRAPHY

Alyssa Pizer
MANAGEMENT
ALYSSAPIZER.COM • ALYSSA@ALYSSAPIZER.COM • 310.440.3930

BAUME NETTOYANT

douceur revitalisante
éclat sublimé

revitalizing softness
sublime radiance

Yves Saint Laurent

coolife by carole & pauline

Colette de Barros

represented by Alyssa Pizer
www.alyssapizer.com
(310) 440-3930
alyssa@alyssapizer.com

DON DIAZ!

Represented by Alyssa Pizer Management www.alyssapizer.com
(310) 310.440.3930 alyssa@alyssapizer.com

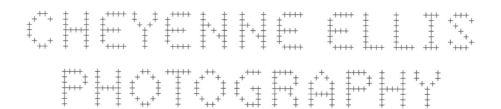

CHEYENNE ELLIS PHOTOGRAPHY

WWW.CHEYENNEELLIS.COM

WILLIAM **GARRETT**
PHOTOGRAPHY

SHANNON_greer_ **PHOTOGRAPHY**

alyssa pizer management
www.alyssapizer.com
310.440.3930
alyssa@alyssapizer.com

REPRESENTED BY / ALYSSA PIZER MANAGEMENT

ALYSSAPIZER.COM / 310 440 3930
ALYSSA@ALYSSAPIZER.COM

185

BRYAN REGAN PHOTOGRAPHY · 919-829-0960 · bryanreganphotography.com
represented by Wonderful Machine

BRYAN REGAN PHOTOGRAPHY · 919-829-0960 · bryanreganphotography.com
represented by Wonderful Machine

alliecottrill

kids tweens & teens

cottrilldesign@comcast.net
www.allisoncottrillphotography.com

KYLE DREIER | www.dreier.com

POBY
PHOTOGRAPHER - DIRECTOR

WWW.POBY.NET

USA: CPi REPS PAM@CPi-REPS.COM 212.683.1455
EUROPE: FROEHLICH MANAGEMENT FROEHLICH@FILM-MANAGEMENT +49.69.2710.8960

EWERT

kate & company

katherine hennessy
617.549.9872
katecompany@gmail.com
www.kate-company.com

rodney rascona
topher cox
carrie prophett
john earle
joshua weinfeld
eric kulin
jim scherer

▼ erickulin.com

▼ rascona.com

▲ tophercox.com

▲ jimscherer.com

▲ carrieprophett.com

▲ johnearlephoto.com

▲ joshuaweinfeld.com

kate & company

JIM SCHERER

PHOTOGRAPHY

www.jimscherer.com

Represented by Kate & Company 617.549.9872 kate@jimscherer.com

represented by Kate & Company
www.kate-company.com
617-549-9872

joshua *weinfeld*

p h o t o g r a p h e r

music

faces

wanderlust

athletics

joshuaweinfeld.com

Represented by
Kate & Company
www.Kate-Company.com
617.549.9872

9/14/11 7:59 AM

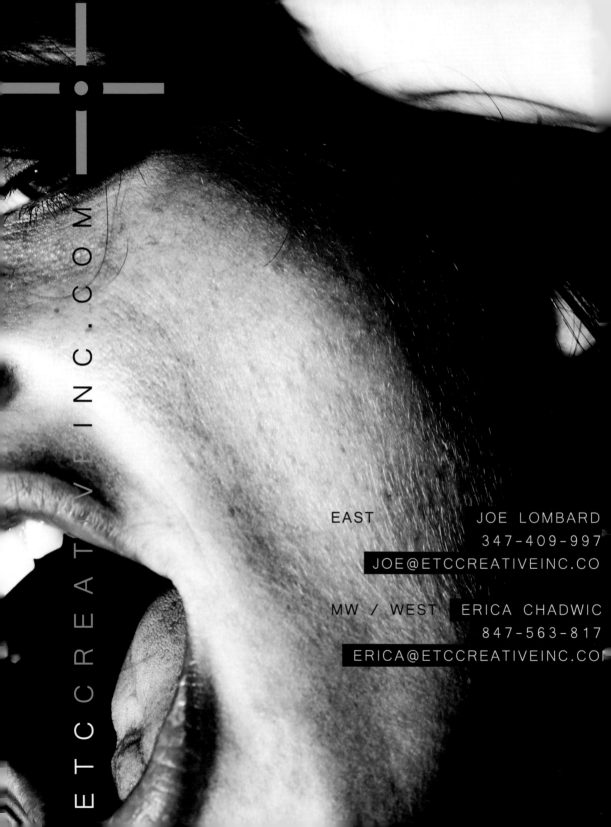

ETCCREATIVEINC.COM

EAST JOE LOMBARD
 347-409-997
JOE@ETCCREATIVEINC.CO

MW / WEST ERICA CHADWIC
 847-563-817
ERICA@ETCCREATIVEINC.CO

PHOTOGRAPHY MOTION INTEGRATED

THOMAS CHADWICK

"IT'S FOOTBALL

NOT SOCCER"

WWW.ETCCREATIVEINC.COM – EAST: 347-409-9973 – MW/WEST: 847-563-8178

THOMAS CHADWICK

"IN YOUR

FACE."

WWW.ETCCREATIVEINC.COM - EAST: 347-409-9973 - MW/WEST: 847-563-817

ARY BADASS"

PASSION

CHRIS CASSIDY

"I WANNA

EAT

"THAT"

WWW.ETCCREATIVEINC.COM – EAST: 347-409-9973 – MW/WEST: 847-563-8178

"EVERYTHING

IS

WITH

BETTER BACON"

WWW.ETCCREATIVEINC.COM – EAST: 347-409-9973 – MW/WEST: 847-563-8178

AARON WARKOV

"IT'S

IN THE

MOMENT"

"I'M 93% RODEO CLOWN,

ralph smith | photographer

Sean Williams
312.421.0100
seanwill.com

S/W

emissary

photography
WINKLER + NOAH
TIM TADDER
MARK LUINENBURG
DAVE JORDANO
DAN GOLDBERG

illustration
PAUL SOMERS
KEVIN SOMERS

LIZ BAUGHER
EMISSARYARTISTS.COM
773.489.9888

Mark Luinenburg

emissary & | LIZ BAUGHER 773.489.9888 EMISSARYARTISTS.COM | WWW.MARKLUINENBURG.COM

Dan Goldberg

Dan Goldberg

emissary & LIZ BAUGHER 773.489.9888 EMISSARYARTISTS.COM | GOLDBERGPHOTOGRAPHY.COM

Tim Tadder

Winkler + Noah

emissary

photography
WINKLER + NOAH
TIM TADDER
MARK LUINENBURG
DAVE JORDANO
DAN GOLDBERG

illustration
PAUL SOMERS
KEVIN SOMERS

LIZ BAUGHER
EMISSARYARTISTS.COM
773.489.9888

DENNIS WELSH

PHOTOGRAPHY and MOTION WWW.DENNISWELSH.COM (207) 846-1130

SANDRO

SAVERIO TRUGLIA

STEPHEN HAMILTON

S|&|C

JOE WIGDAHL

MARK WIENS

schumann & company / 312.925.1530 / www.schumannco.com

S|&|C STEPHEN HAMILTON

S|&|C

TERRY VINE

schumann & company / 312.925.1530 / www.schumannco.com

S|&|C SAVERIO TRUGLIA

S / & / C

MARK WIENS

schumann & company / 312.925.1530 / www.schumannco.com

jason**LINDSEY**.com

DIRECTOR and PHOTOGRAPHER | 800-898-7617

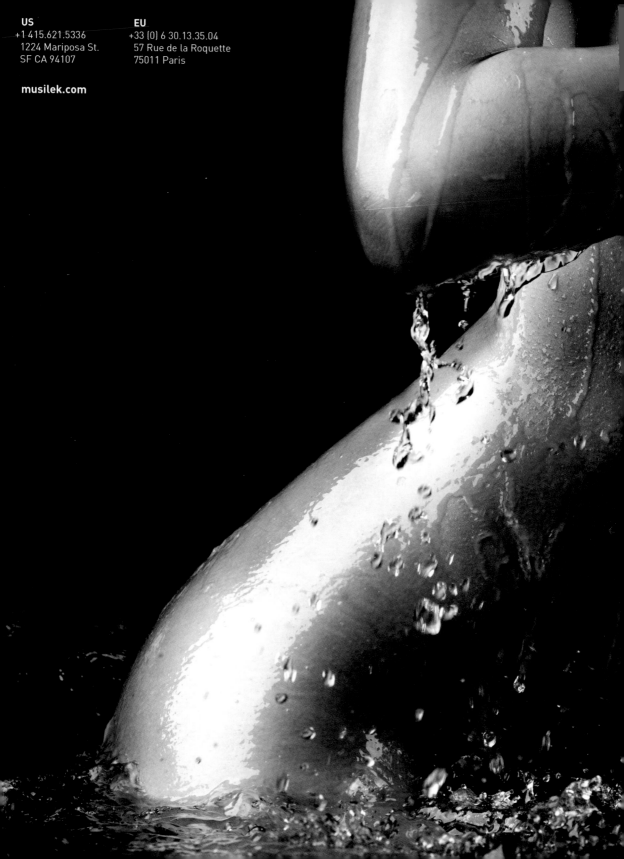

musilek

LÜNING/PHOTO

luningphoto.com 312.953.0869

billcahill

billcahill.com 310-497-3567

stewartcohen**pictures**

STEVE
LESNICK

PHOTOGRAPHY

stevelesnick.com
agent:dougtruppe.com

Henrique Bagulho

Sue Barr

David Bishop

Kan Nakai

Robert Randall

Gandee Vasan

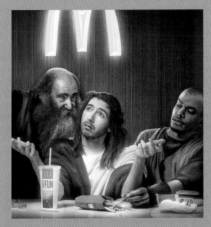

Clor

Darrell Eager

Michael Weschler

Bret Wills

WSW creative 212-431-4480 | wswcreative.com | henriquebagulho.com

SUE BARR

DAVID BISHOP

WSW East: Represented by WSW Creative | 212-431-4480 | robert-randall.co

WS+W creative 212-431-4480 | wswcreative.com | gandeevasan.com

GANDEE VASAN

MICHAEL WESCHLER

JIMMY WILLIAMS

PHOTOGRAPHY

Life

Luxe

Faces

Places

www.JimmyWilliamsPhotography.com

919-832-5971

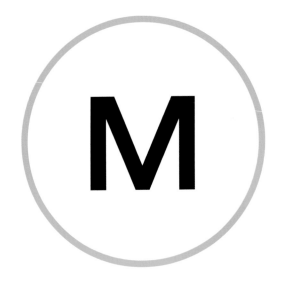

M REPRESENTS, INC. 212 840 8100

ACT TWO|UM/CGI & Retouching JIM HUIBREGTSE/Still Life & Liquids
ALICE BLUE/CGI & Illustration GARY SALTER/Conceptual & Humor
JENNY RISHER/Beauty, Fashion, & Portrait JULIE GANG/Kids-Babies
DENIS WAUGH/Locations & People RAY MASSEY/Liquids-Splash
JAMES PORTO/Photo-Illustration CONRAD PIEPENBURG/Automotive
FERNANDO MILANI/Beauty-Hair, Skin & Body/MREPRESENTS.COM

FERNANDO MILANI
represented by
M REPRESENTS INC
212 840 8100
ralph@mrepresents.com

GARY SALTER
represented by
M REPRESENTS INC
212 840 8100
ralph@mrepresents.com

James Porto

vgpictures.com 214.284.0018
represented by Those 3 Reps 800.579.0807

Vanessa Gavalya
PICTURES

AWARDS

Communication Arts Photography Annual 2011
Archive's 200 Best Ad Photographers Worldwide 2010
Archive's 200 Best Ad Photographers Worldwide 2009
Graphis Photo 2009 Sports
Graphis Photo 2008 Landscape
Graphis Photo 2008 Landscape
American Photography 2008
Graphis Photo 2007 Wildlife
Graphis Photo 2007 People
Workbook inspiration page 2007
2006 Gold Addy Award
Graphis Design Annual 2006
Communication Arts Exhibit 2006 May/June
2006 Lucie Award Nature-Underwater Professional
2005 IPA Photo Award People in Professional
2005 IPA Photo Award Advertising in Professional
Workbook inspiration page 2005
Graphis Photo 2004 landscape
Graphis Photo 2004 Sports
Applied Arts Photography and Illustration Annual 2004
Applied Arts Photography and Illustration Annual 2004
Archive Magazine Vol 5 2003
2003 Altpick Award (c)
2003 Altpick Award (b)
2003 Altpick Award (a)
AdNews 2003
Communication Arts Photography Annual 2003
Communication Arts Exhibit Online 2003
Communication Arts Exhibit, March/April 2002
Graphis Photo Gallery (issue 348)
2002 Gold Addy Award
2002 Silver Addy Award (b)
2002 Silver Addy Award (a)
32nd International Underwater Photo competition,1st place
APA 2001
Graphis Photo 1996

PAOLO **MARCHESI**

Photography

MONTANA 406 _ _____ 5806040
SAN FRANCISCO 415 _ _____ 7382074

WWW.MARCHESIPHOTO.COM

Leigh Beisch

David Martin

Kevin Twomey

Ann Elliott Cutting

Jim Smiths

Richard Schultz

Hunter Freeman

Ron Berg

Andy Anderson

hunter@hunterfreeman.com
415 252 1910 phone
www.hunterfreeman.com
hunterfreeman.wordpress.com

Represented by
Heather Elder
415 931 7709 phone
www.heatherelder.com
elderrep.wordpress.com

Visit www.heatherelderstock.com

heather elder

david martinez

DONALD
GRAHAM

DONALD GRAHAM

www.donaldgraham.com
Represented by Daniele Forsythe Photographers
New York 212 693 7470 Los Angeles 310 450 1650

Andrea Rugg

Photography

Jeff Baker
Brian Coats
Fernando Decillis
Michael Haskins
Paolo Marchesi
Jeff Moore
Andrea Rugg

Illustration/3d

Duarte Imaging
Greg McCullough

Fernando Decillis

Paolo Marchesi

Michael Haskins

Michael Haskins

Paolo Marchesi

Brian Coats

Jeff Moore

Jeff Bakken

SCOTT MONTGOMERY
smontgomery.com

Lisa Button
buttonrepresents.com

TADD MYERS

SEE MORE AT

TADDMYERS.COM

AMERICANCRAFTSMANPROJECT.COM

A Niels Van Iperen **B** Satoshi **C** Steve Beaudet **D** Dennis Murphy **E** Ross Whitaker **F** Kevin Arnold **G** Leland Bobbé **H** Lorenz + Avelar

RBR

ROBERT
BACALL
REPRESENTATIVES

L

K

M

BACALL.COM

917.763.6554 · ROB@BACALL.COM · PHOTOGRAPHYMOTIONSGI · FINDISON in

I Sam Robles **J** Robb Scharetg **K** Andrew Hall **L** Eric Van Den Brulle **M** Terry Heffernan

Veruca Honeyscotch

ROBERT
BACALL
REPRESENTATIVES

917.763.6554

Dottie Lux

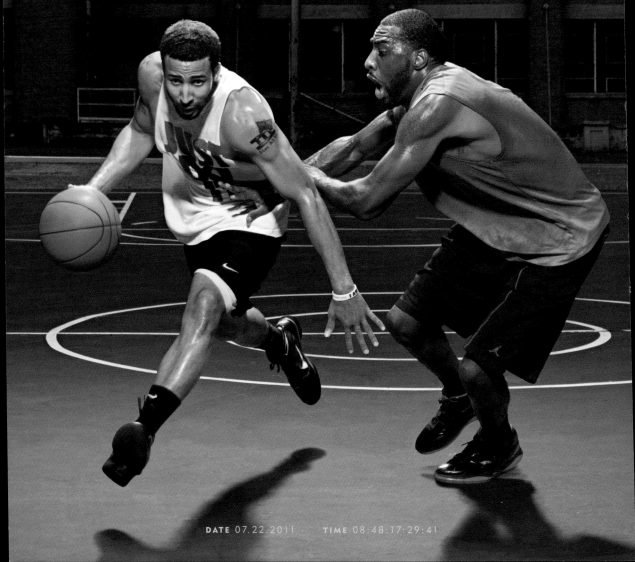

ROBB SCHARETG

[PICTURES]

ROBB SCHARETG

[PICTURES]

CamilleTokerudPhotography

917 821-9881 . New York, NY . ctokerud@mac.com . www.camilletokerud.com

BIL
ZEL
MAN
PHOT
OGRA
PHER

zelmanstudios.com

represented by
@Radical Media

represented by
Sherry Riad 212.797.0009

r. Quackenbush
www.russquackenbush.com

CREATIVE MANAGEMENT AT mc²

PHOTOGRAPHY | NEW YORK | MIAMI
646.638.3321 | www.creativemanagementmc2.com

REPRESENTING:

KEITH LATHROP

GRE**GH**INSDALE

REPRESENTED BY CREATIVE MANAGEMENT AT MC2
WWW.CREATIVEMANAGEMENTMC2.COM
NEW YORK | 646.638.3321

Izod :: Death Valley, CA

MichaelVoorhees.com
studio: 949.650.6150

CARLIDAVIDSO

BRADGUIC

PAUL**ARESU**
PHOTO / MOTION

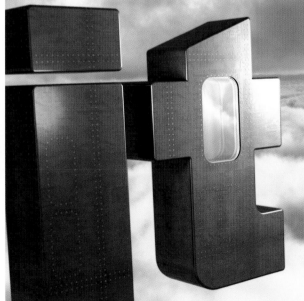

ROBERT**TARDIO**
PHOTO

ALTER
CGI / MOTION / PHOTO

2FAKE
CGI / MOTION

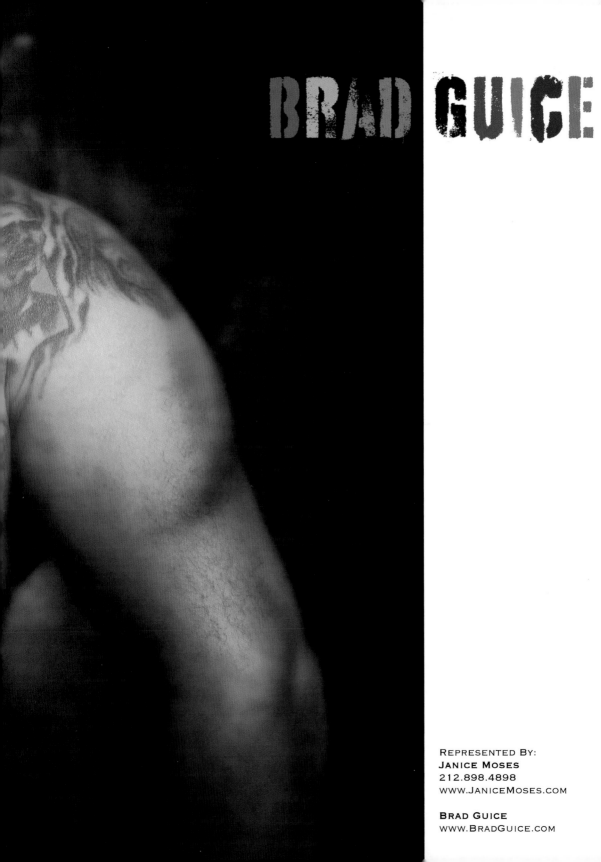

BRAD GUICE

REPRESENTED BY:
JANICE MOSES
212.898.4898
WWW.JANICEMOSES.COM

BRAD GUICE
WWW.BRADGUICE.COM

BRILLIANT

is cinema quality entertainment at the speed of 4G.

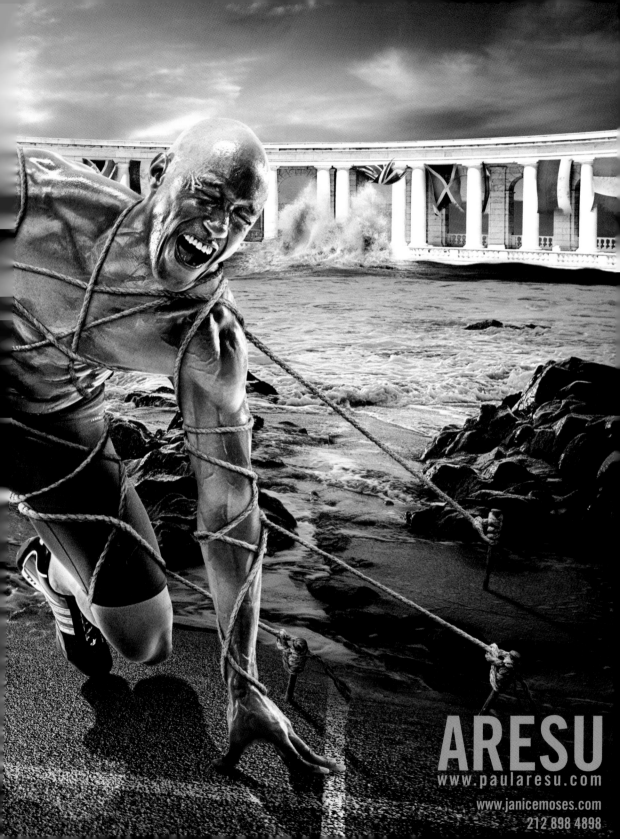

ARESU
www.paularesu.com

www.janicemoses.com
212 898 4898

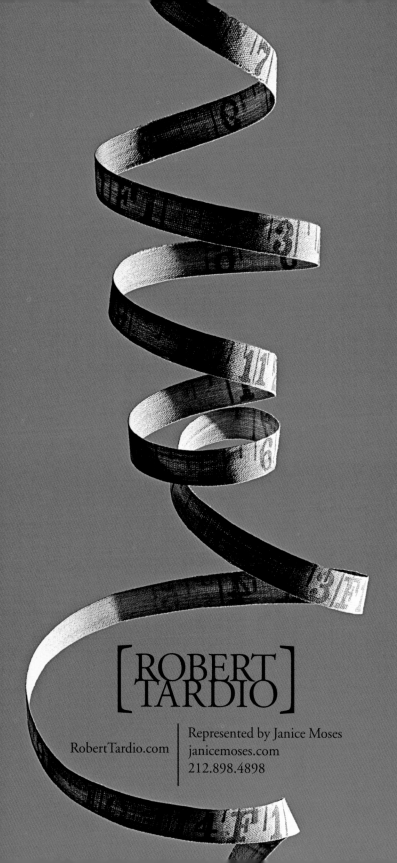

[ROBERT]
[TARDIO]

RobertTardio.com

Represented by Janice Moses
janicemoses.com
212.898.4898

CHRIS CRISMAN

Photographer

CHRIS CRISMAN

Photographer

381

CHRIS CRISMAN
Photographer